P9-DMJ-132

Horses

by Martha E. H. Rustad

Consulting Editor: Gail Saunders-Smith, Ph.D.

Consultant: Jennifer Zablotny, D.V.M.,
Member, American Animal Hospital Association

Pebble Books

an imprint of Capstone Press
Mankato, Minnesota

Pebble Books are published by Capstone Press
151 Good Counsel Drive, P.O. Box 669, Mankato, Minnesota 56002
http://www.capstone-press.com

1 2 3 4 5 6 07 06 05 04 03 02

Library of Congress Cataloging-in-Publication Data
Rustad, Martha E. H. (Martha Elizabeth Hillman), 1975–
    Horses / by Martha E. H. Rustad.
    p. cm.—(All about pets)
    Includes bibliographical references (p. 23) and index.
    ISBN 0-7368-0976-7
    1. Horses—Juvenile literature. [1. Horses.] I. Title. II. All about pets (Mankato,
Minn.)
SF302 .R87 2002
636.1—dc21
                                                                2001000259

Summary: Simple text and photographs introduce and illustrate horses, their
features, and basic care.

Note to Parents and Teachers

The All About Pets series supports national science standards for
units on the diversity and unity of life. This book describes horses
and illustrates what they need from their owners. The photographs
support emergent readers in understanding the text. The repetition
of words and phrases helps emergent readers learn new words.
This book also introduces emergent readers to subject-specific
vocabulary words, which are defined in the Words to Know section.
Emergent readers may need assistance to read some words and to
use the Table of Contents, Words to Know, Read More, Internet
Sites, and Index/Word List sections of the book.

Table of Contents

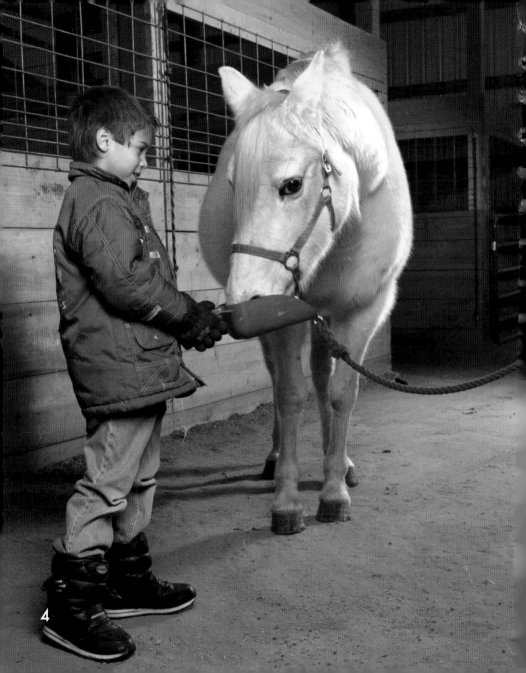

Some horses are pets.

mane

Horses have a mane.

Horses have big teeth.

Horses have long legs.

hooves

Horses have hooves.

14

Horses need a lot of food and water.

Horses need
a clean stable.

Horses need
to be brushed often.

Horses need room to run.

Words to Know

brush—to smooth hair using an object with bristles and a handle; pet owners should brush a horse's coat and mane every day.

food—something that people, animals, and plants need to stay alive; horses eat oats, grass, and hay.

hoof—the hard covering over the foot of a horse; horses wear horseshoes on their hooves; pet owners must clean horses' hooves every day.

mane—the long, thick hair on the head and neck of a horse

pet—a tame animal kept for company or pleasure; only certain kinds of horses should be kept as pets; wild horses do not make good pets.

stable—a building where horses are kept; pet owners should clean horse stables every day.

teeth—the white, bony parts of a mouth; horses bite and chew food with their teeth.

Read More

Bell, Rachael. *Horses.* Farm Animals. Chicago: Heinemann Library, 2000.

Budd, Jackie. *Horse and Pony Care.* Complete Guides to Horses and Ponies. Milwaukee: Gareth Stevens, 1998.

Miller, Heather. *My Horses.* My Farm. New York: Children's Press, 2000.

Internet Sites

Horse Printout
http://www.enchantedlearning.com/subjects/mammals/horse/Horsecoloring.shtml

Horses
http://www.kidsfarm.com/horses.htm

Silverstone Riders Club
http://www.silverstoneriders.co.uk

Index/Word List

Word Count: 43
Early-Intervention Level: 6

Credits
Kia Bielke, cover designer and illustrator; Kimberly Danger, photo researcher

Capstone Press/Gary Sundermeyer, 4, 8, 16, 18
David F. Clobes, Stock Photography, 20
Dusty L. Perin, 6, 12, 14 (both)
International Stock/Richard Pharaoh, 1; Caroline Wood, 10
Photri-Microstock, cover

Special thanks to Stoney Ridge Stable, Mankato, Minnesota, for their help with
photo shoots.